The life of faith in death, in
expectation of the resurrection
from the dead opened in a
sermon at the funerall of the right
worshipfull Mr. Thomas Slany
late maior of the famous town
and corporation of King-Lynn
in the county of Norfolk (1649)

John Horn

The life of faith in death, in expectation of the resurrection from the dead opened in a sermon at the funerall of the right worshipfull Mr. Thomas Slany late maior of the famous town and corporation of King-Lynn in the county of Norfolk

Horn, John, 1614-1676.
[4], 30 [1] p.
London : Printed by Abraham Miller ..., 1649.
Wing / H2804
English
Reproduction of the original in the Cambridge University Library

Early English Books Online (EEBO) Editions

Imagine holding history in your hands.

Now you can. Digitally preserved and previously accessible only through libraries as Early English Books Online, this rare material is now available in single print editions. Thousands of books written between 1475 and 1700 and ranging from religion to astronomy, medicine to music, can be delivered to your doorstep in individual volumes of high-quality historical reproductions.

We have been compiling these historic treasures for more than 70 years. Long before such a thing as "digital" even existed, ProQuest founder Eugene Power began the noble task of preserving the British Museum's collection on microfilm. He then sought out other rare and endangered titles, providing unparalleled access to these works and collaborating with the world's top academic institutions to make them widely available for the first time. This project furthers that original vision.

These texts have now made the full journey -- from their original printing-press versions available only in rare-book rooms to online library access to new single volumes made possible by the partnership between artifact preservation and modern printing technology. A portion of the proceeds from every book sold supports the libraries and institutions that made this collection possible, and that still work to preserve these invaluable treasures passed down through time.

This is history, traveling through time since the dawn of printing to your own personal library.

Initial Proquest EEBO Print Editions collections include:

Early Literature

This comprehensive collection begins with the famous Elizabethan Era that saw such literary giants as Chaucer, Shakespeare and Marlowe, as well as the introduction of the sonnet. Traveling through Jacobean and Restoration literature, the highlight of this series is the Pollard and Redgrave 1475-1640 selection of the rarest works from the English Renaissance.

Early Documents of World History

This collection combines early English perspectives on world history with documentation of Parliament records, royal decrees and military documents that reveal the delicate balance of Church and State in early English government. For social historians, almanacs and calendars offer insight into daily life of common citizens. This exhaustively complete series presents a thorough picture of history through the English Civil War.

Historical Almanacs

Historically, almanacs served a variety of purposes from the more practical, such as planting and harvesting crops and plotting nautical routes, to predicting the future through the movements of the stars. This collection provides a wide range of consecutive years of "almanacks" and calendars that depict a vast array of everyday life as it was several hundred years ago.

Early History of Astronomy & Space

Humankind has studied the skies for centuries, seeking to find our place in the universe. Some of the most important discoveries in the field of astronomy were made in these texts recorded by ancient stargazers, but almost as impactful were the perspectives of those who considered their discoveries to be heresy. Any independent astronomer will find this an invaluable collection of titles arguing the truth of the cosmic system.

Early History of Industry & Science

Acting as a kind of historical Wall Street, this collection of industry manuals and records explores the thriving industries of construction; textile, especially wool and linen; salt; livestock; and many more.

Early English Wit, Poetry & Satire

The power of literary device was never more in its prime than during this period of history, where a wide array of political and religious satire mocked the status quo and poetry called humankind to transcend the rigors of daily life through love, God or principle. This series comments on historical patterns of the human condition that are still visible today.

Early English Drama & Theatre

This collection needs no introduction, combining the works of some of the greatest canonical writers of all time, including many plays composed for royalty such as Queen Elizabeth I and King Edward VI. In addition, this series includes history and criticism of drama, as well as examinations of technique.

Early History of Travel & Geography

Offering a fascinating view into the perception of the world during the sixteenth and seventeenth centuries, this collection includes accounts of Columbus's discovery of the Americas and encompasses most of the Age of Discovery, during which Europeans and their descendants intensively explored and mapped the world. This series is a wealth of information from some the most groundbreaking explorers.

Early Fables & Fairy Tales

This series includes many translations, some illustrated, of some of the most well-known mythologies of today, including Aesop's Fables and English fairy tales, as well as many Greek, Latin and even Oriental parables and criticism and interpretation on the subject.

Early Documents of Language & Linguistics

The evolution of English and foreign languages is documented in these original texts studying and recording early philology from the study of a variety of languages including Greek, Latin and Chinese, as well as multilingual volumes, to current slang and obscure words. Translations from Latin, Hebrew and Aramaic, grammar treatises and even dictionaries and guides to translation make this collection rich in cultures from around the world.

Early History of the Law

With extensive collections of land tenure and business law "forms" in Great Britain, this is a comprehensive resource for all kinds of early English legal precedents from feudal to constitutional law, Jewish and Jesuit law, laws about public finance to food supply and forestry, and even "immoral conditions." An abundance of law dictionaries, philosophy and history and criticism completes this series.

Early History of Kings, Queens and Royalty

This collection includes debates on the divine right of kings, royal statutes and proclamations, and political ballads and songs as related to a number of English kings and queens, with notable concentrations on foreign rulers King Louis IX and King Louis XIV of France, and King Philip II of Spain. Writings on ancient rulers and royal tradition focus on Scottish and Roman kings, Cleopatra and the Biblical kings Nebuchadnezzar and Solomon.

Early History of Love, Marriage & Sex

Human relationships intrigued and baffled thinkers and writers well before the postmodern age of psychology and self-help. Now readers can access the insights and intricacies of Anglo-Saxon interactions in sex and love, marriage and politics, and the truth that lies somewhere in between action and thought.

Early History of Medicine, Health & Disease

This series includes fascinating studies on the human brain from as early as the 16th century, as well as early studies on the physiological effects of tobacco use. Anatomy texts, medical treatises and wound treatment are also discussed, revealing the exponential development of medical theory and practice over more than two hundred years.

Early History of Logic, Science and Math

The "hard sciences" developed exponentially during the 16th and 17th centuries, both relying upon centuries of tradition and adding to the foundation of modern application, as is evidenced by this extensive collection. This is a rich collection of practical mathematics as applied to business, carpentry and geography as well as explorations of mathematical instruments and arithmetic; logic and logicians such as Aristotle and Socrates; and a number of scientific disciplines from natural history to physics.

Early History of Military, War and Weaponry

Any professional or amateur student of war will thrill at the untold riches in this collection of war theory and practice in the early Western World. The Age of Discovery and Enlightenment was also a time of great political and religious unrest, revealed in accounts of conflicts such as the Wars of the Roses.

Early History of Food

This collection combines the commercial aspects of food handling, preservation and supply to the more specific aspects of canning and preserving, meat carving, brewing beer and even candy-making with fruits and flowers, with a large resource of cookery and recipe books. Not to be forgotten is a "the great eater of Kent," a study in food habits.

Early History of Religion

From the beginning of recorded history we have looked to the heavens for inspiration and guidance. In these early religious documents, sermons, and pamphlets, we see the spiritual impact on the lives of both royalty and the commoner. We also get insights into a clergy that was growing ever more powerful as a political force. This is one of the world's largest collections of religious works of this type, revealing much about our interpretation of the modern church and spirituality.

Early Social Customs

Social customs, human interaction and leisure are the driving force of any culture. These unique and quirky works give us a glimpse of interesting aspects of day-to-day life as it existed in an earlier time. With books on games, sports, traditions, festivals, and hobbies it is one of the most fascinating collections in the series.

The BiblioLife Network

This project was made possible in part by the BiblioLife Network (BLN), a project aimed at addressing some of the huge challenges facing book preservationists around the world. The BLN includes libraries, library networks, archives, subject matter experts, online communities and library service providers. We believe every book ever published should be available as a high-quality print reproduction; printed on-demand anywhere in the world. This insures the ongoing accessibility of the content and helps generate sustainable revenue for the libraries and organizations that work to preserve these important materials.

The following book is in the "public domain" and represents an authentic reproduction of the text as printed by the original publisher. While we have attempted to accurately maintain the integrity of the original work, there are sometimes problems with the original work or the micro-film from which the books were digitized. This can result in minor errors in reproduction. Possible imperfections include missing and blurred pages, poor pictures, markings and other reproduction issues beyond our control. Because this work is culturally important, we have made it available as part of our commitment to protecting, preserving, and promoting the world's literature.

GUIDE TO FOLD-OUTS MAPS and OVERSIZED IMAGES

The book you are reading was digitized from microfilm captured over the past thirty to forty years. Years after the creation of the original microfilm, the book was converted to digital files and made available in an online database.

In an online database, page images do not need to conform to the size restrictions found in a printed book. When converting these images back into a printed bound book, the page sizes are standardized in ways that maintain the detail of the original. For large images, such as fold-out maps, the original page image is split into two or more pages

Guidelines used to determine how to split the page image follows:

- Some images are split vertically; large images require vertical and horizontal splits.
- For horizontal splits, the content is split left to right.
- For vertical splits, the content is split from top to bottom.
- For both vertical and horizontal splits, the image is processed from top left to bottom right.

cm 1 2 3 4 5 6 7 8 9 10 11 12 13 14 15 16 17 18 19

THE
LIFE OF FAITH
IN
DEATH,

In expectation of the Resurrection
from the DEAD.

Opened in a Sermon at the Funerall
of the Right Worshipfull Mr *Thomas Slany*
late Maior of the famous Town and Corporation
of *Kings-Lynn* in the County of *Norfolk*, who decea-
sed in the year of his Maioralty, *Jan.* 10. 1649.

PREACHED THERE

By JOHN HORN an unworthy Servant of God, in the
Gospel of his Sonne Jesus Christ, whereof he is a
Preacher to the Congregation at *Lynn Allhallows*.

HEBREWS 6. 12.

*Be not slothfull, but follow the steps of those who through faith and
patience have inherited the promises.*

HOSEA 13. 14.

*I will ransome them from the power of the grave, I will redeem them
from death, O death, I will be thy plague, O grave, I will be thy
destruction, repentance is hid from mine eyes.*

Fiducia Christianorum Resurrectio mortuorum, Contemplatio est spei in hoc
spacio, non praesentatio, expectatio, non possessio. *Tertul. de Res Carnis.*

Hæc fidei vis est, quòd mediat inter vitam & mortem, & mortem transmutat
in vitam. *Luther.*

LONDON,
Printed by *Abraham Miller* dwelling in *Black-friers.* 1649.

Mrs. MARY SLANY

Relict of the late Worshipfull

Mr Thomas Slany, with his and their
Children, Grace, Mercy and Peace,
from God our Father, and
our Lord Jesus Christ.

Beloved,   14 — 201

AT your motion and by your request these papers are become more publike then was intended: not for any rare worth in them, but to satis-
fie your desire and esteem of them, which though at first I was more
inclinable to, considering that they bear some testimony, though not
much, against some spreading evils of these times, yet upon second
thoughts I began to recoil, and should have contented my self with your private enjoyment of them, considering the plenty of books, and the slanderresse of what these
contain, and what the temper of the world is, that they would be ready to laugh at
and deride my doings, and accuse me of arrogancy and foolishnesse: of arrogancy as
if I sought to be known and taken notice of, of foolishnesse in endeavouring it ly (or
in filling the world with) such dead discourses, and this had stifled it in its birth,
and made it never for me to have seen the Sun in this way, had not my respect to
you and your desire, made me to disregard these reasonings, which yet it did with
some reluctancy, while I further considered, that as my weaknesse would provoke
some to sleght the witnesse born against their evils, so my plainnesse might perhaps
offend others, and engage them against me into some contentions, not which, but
their bettering and profit is my desire: but Gods will be done in it, he is a free agent
and can do all things, and oftentimes worketh by most unlikely means, and doth most
good where least is expected. One talent put to the improvement may bring forth a
second withl is blessing on it, and though some may hurt themselves, yet others more
sober minded may happily pick something from it that may serve to their profit, yea,
some perhaps may finde leisure to look on such a Paper who either want it for, or
money to procure larger volumes: for your sakes then and for theirs I have adventu-
red it to publike censure.

And seeing you were so much his whose sur erall this solemnized, To you it's meet-
est in the first place with these portions of himself he hath left surviving him, that
I commend it, not to provoke you to renewed grief in thought of your losse of him,
but to stir you up to imitate his vertues in minding his gains by them May you, his
and yours be so mingled hereby of his or those for er worthies faith and walkings, as
thereby to be stirred up to receive embrace and where you have embraced to hold fast
the word and promises, and so to follow their vertuous footsteps in contempt of the
world, an earnest pursuit of the promised rest as to live by faith and die in faith:
I shall think my labor herein well bestowed, whose hearty prayer is your prosperities,
subscribing my self with my endeavours,

Yours, to serve you

in the Gospel of Christ,

J. H.

To the Right Worſhipfull

Mʳ THOMAS REVET

Maior of the Town and Corporation of
Lynn in Norfolk, with his worſhipfull Bre-
thren and Aſſiſtants, Grace and
Mercy in Chriſt Jeſus.

Right Worſhipfull,

I Am bold to preſent you with theſe Papers, becauſe you were not only audi-
tors of, but alſo much intereſſed in what they contain, they preſent you with
a memoriall of a late head of yours, though untimely (as to your wiſhed benefit by him) cut off by the hand of death, providence ſo ordering that the
leſſer body ſhould therein be the præludium and forerunning repreſentation
of a greater, of whom you bear the image and ſuperſcription: what was wan-
ting to his honour here by the ſhortneſſe of his Maioralty, I have endeavoured herein to ſupply, by adding to his memory, which though he need not for himſelf, yet in ſome
thing, may be uſefull for us, ſomething it may afford us for inſtruction, ſomething for imitation.
He was a man of parts, that's known I think to all of us, and yet I have heard intelligent men
ſay they were known to few; what they were would beſt have appeared in their improvement :
but before you and he came to that point (as to Magiſtracy) he and they too were almoſt
gone : there is ſomething in that worthy of our inſtruction; when God gives you men of parts,
make uſe of them (as to office) while ye may enjoy them, chiefly ſuch as are alſo exemplary
for piety, and worthy imitation: and ſuch as have parts, be ye willing to improve them while ye
have opportunity *Poſt eſt occaſio calva.*

When God preſents us with a mercy, it's wiſdom to meet it in the face, and not let it ſlide
by us, till it be paſt recovery. He was a man of integrity, mercy, piety, one that affected ho-
neſtly more then his honour, in theſe things he was worthy imitation. It's wiſdom (ſo far as we
may) to imitate in our ſelves whatſoever we are convinced of is good in others But have theſe
Papers nothing elſe but a mention of him? perhaps your wiſdoms may pick out ſomething elſe,
though through my little ability but weakly handled, yet that may afford ſome ſpirituall profit.
If it be but to put you in minde of death: that's worth the thinking of. that well conſidered may
make you the better while you live, but indeed there are ſome other things that inclined me to
the publiſhing it, chiefly the witneſſe herein born againſt a th eefold ſpreading and overcommon
malady, one that denies the extent of the Goſpel-doctrine of the death of Chriſt, and good
will of God to ſinners, ſomething akinne to the old Phariſaiſm, that would tie it up to the elect,
the Jews and people proſelyted into themſelves, whom they therefore alſo judged of
the ſame election with themſelves : denying it to Publicans and ſinners not ſo regulated,
and to uncircumciſed gentile (the body and generality of them) not ſo proſelyted. The
ſecond is the common profanneſſe of ſuperficiall Chriſtians and turners of the grace and Go-
ſpel of Chriſt into wantonneſs, that reſt in a name and notion of Chriſtianity, but deny the power of it, of which ſort there are every where too many, The third is the ſect of the Sadduces,
that deny the reſurrection, the viſible coming of Chriſt perſonally again, and the glorious performance of the promiſes at that his appearing, a too too ſpreading generation. May God make
it uſefull to you to ſeade you beſides all theſe rocks, in the true ancient Scripture-doctrine and
faith formerly alſo atteſted to in the Church in England, ſo to embrace and love the promiſed
ſalvation, and ſo to follow the ſteps of this good man, and of other Worthies that have gone
before him, in the belief of and hearty love to, cloſing with an entertainment of the Word
of God, that it may produce like fruits in you as in them, unto death and in death, that you with
them alſo may partake of the glorious reſurrection unto life and happineſſe, I ſhall have cauſe
of much rejoicing : The fountain of mercy and wiſdom flow down upon you, fill you with truth,
with peace and righteouſneſſe, direct and bleſſe you, and make you bleſſings in your places and
generations, So praieth,

Your Worſhips Servant
to his ability,

J. H.

A 2

Vpon the ſubject of this Book,

An Instruction and Hymn.

Reader, ſee here how great a myſtery
Lies wrapped up in Chriſtianity.
Strange Paradoxes! here's a buſh o flame
Burning yet not conſumed by the ſame,
By Coll quintida death in the ſet,
And yet ſo heal'd that it killeth not,
Drink from a rock, in gravell wholſome ſeed,
In darkneſſe light, in midſt of evil good,
In ſickneſſe health, the ſweeteſt eaſe in pain,
In weakneſſe ſtrength, in loſſe the greateſt gain,
Yea life in death, and in abſurdities
The depth of wiſdom, baffling all the niſe.
That tell how men by falling riſe, and how
By loſing what they have they richer grows
How by diſhonour men may mount on high,
By being overcome have victory.
Here haſt thou meat out of the eater, here
Sweet from the ſtrong, boldneſſe in greateſt fear,
A dying man ſtill full of life and breath,
Conquer'd and yet triumphing over death,
But whence all this? or how can theſe things be?
Shall Paradoxes be Divinity?
Behold, here's God with man, Emmanuel,
That only word that riddle doth unſpell.
In God is good, light is all ſtrength eaſe and gain
In man ill, darkneſſe, ſickneſſe, weakneſſe, pain,
Terſorrow loſſe, and miſery, and death,
God fountain of bliſſe, joy, life and breath,
In Chriſt theſe meet, Behold the myſtery,
Manhood united with the Deity.
Yea, all theſe properties and conſequents
Of each, found place in him: a battell thence
In him was fought, while ſin on righteouſneſſe,
Death on eternall life, and curſe on bleſſe,
Made their aſſault, for theſe on him did ſeiſe,
Cauſe God to bruiſe his precious ſoul did
Diſplaying there his glory, for on God (pleaſe,
Death with its train could finde but ſmall abode,
Though the humanity did yeeld thereto,
The Deity from reſcued is therefro.
And ſince our evils in that death did meet.
The eater yeelded meat, and the ſtrong ſweet.
God ſhew'd himſelf in man, in weakneſſe ſtrength,
In darkneſſe glorious light, in ſhortneſſe length,
Even length of daies and immortality,
Death being ſwallowed up in victory,
Of which mans nature being diſpoſſeſt,
Is now become in him Gods endleſſe reſt,

Yea, men is there the ſeat of bleſſings all
Afforded, and captivity made thrall,
Which treaſured are in him for us, from thence
Bleſſings of every kinde God doth diſpenſe.
Chriſt by his holy Word and ſpirit, by which
He peace and pardon in his Name doth preach,
By theſe he worketh faith, and that the uſe
Chriſt us and Chriſt bringing to unitie
With him, from which doth ſuch communion flow
That he and we no longer are as two;
Joyn'd in one ſpirit as he took our fleſh,
So he gives us his Spirit, which doth refreſh
And fill our hearts with joy: Gods power he is
Conquering death and its accompliſh
In us, as once in Chriſt, with whom join'd thus,
He writes his Name upon us, God with us,
He is our life in death, hope in deſpair,
Our ſtrength in weakneſſe, and he doth repair
Our breaches all, while he doth make us ſee
That we ſhall riſe and reign as well as he.
Oh glorious death by which our life appears!
Oh glorious Spirit that our hearts up bears!
Oh glorious Word that doth his tidings bring!
Oh glorious Chriſt where our heavenly King
Comes riding to us meekly, precious Faith
That ſuch a ſpring and ſuch an iſſue hath.
Oh precious Lord that burſts us in ſuch love!
Thy ſelf ſo to abaſe, ill to remove
From us on whom it lay, and would have wrought
Our endleſſe ruine, Thus to us haſt brought
Life, yea, even ſtill life. Thou art the day
That lightneſt our night. Thou art the way
By which God comes to us in his great night,
By which he gave to us his holy Spirit,
By which we come to him and finde his power
Infuſing life into us in deaths hour.
Thou art the Word, on thee the Spirit is put
To open eyes that blinde are, and to ſhut
Theſe ſped ears, from bondage to ſet free,
And to get over death full victory.
Oh ſhew thy ſelf to us, be thou our life,
Fill us with peace and joy, end all our ſtrife,
Be thou our All, open our hearts to ſee,
And fill us with thy glory, ſo ſhall we
Triumph in midſt of death, and ſing thy praiſe,
Full well aſſured that thou then us wilt raiſe
Us up again, and ſet us on thy Throne,
For evermore with God to be at one.

THE
LIFE OF FAITH
IN
DEATH.

The Text.

HEBREWS II. 13,14. *All these died* (κατὰ πίστιν) *in* (or according to) *faith, not having received the promises, but seeing them afar off, they were perswaded, and embraced them, and confessed that they were strangers and sojourners in the earth.*

For they that say such things manifest that they seek a Countrey.

He custome of a solemn interring of the dead bodies of deceased friends, and of making lamentations over them is very ancient and laudable, the mention of it is as old as *Abrahams* time, we finde it was then a custome usuall in the Eastern countries, as we reade in the book of *Genesis* of the Patriarchs and Egyptians, and surely in its original it was *tessera & fides & amoris*, a pledge and testimony both of their faith and love, *fidei*, a witnesse of their faith that they beleeved and looked for the resurrection of the body, and therefore would decently bestow cost upon, and interre the body : *amoris*, of their love to the deceased, whose reliques therefore they so farre honoured, and whose losse (or absence rather) they lamented, as in their presence formerly they had been delighted : thus I might shew you *Abraham* himself the father of the faithfull, *Gen.* 23. 2. burying the Corps of his deceased *Sarah*, and weeping for her, and yet it is observable that the Jews write the letter כ in the word בכה that signifies to weep very small וַיִּבְכֶּה to intimate the practice of *Abraham* to have been sutable to what the Apostle *Paul* expresly wishes that beleevers in the like cases should

be,

be, 1 *Thef.*4 13. a moderate mourning for their dead in the Lord, as those that believing the doctrine of the resurrection, are not without hope for them, I might point you likewise to *Jacobs* buriall of his wife *Rachel*, and his and *Esaus* buriall of their father *Isaac, Gen.* 35.19,20,29. and to *Joseph* and his brethren, with many of the Egyptians, making a very great lamentation for old *Ifrael* when they buried him, insomuch that the place where they staied lamenting him, got from thence a new denomination, being afterward called *Abel Mizraim*, or, the Egyptians mourning. because of the excessive mourning of the Egyptians, by which it seems that the Egyptians though least akinne to him, yet made the greatest lamentation, surely not because they lov_d him better then his children, but because they were not so well instructed, and therefore had neither so much knowledge, nor so much hope of the resurrection which should have put more bounds unto their mourning, except we shall say that the whole company coming out of Egypt had the common name of Egyptians put upon them, because so adjudged to be by the people thereabout inhabiting. I might tell you to, of the interring of *Aaron, Miriam*, and the lamentations made for them, as also for *Moses, Joshua, Samuel*, and many others : but then as the Apostle sayes in this *Heb.*11, in another case, the time would fail me, or my strength would fail me by exceeding the time: I shall therefore content my self with what is said to that, and turn from this discourse to my text, and see what it will afford for our observation and usefullnesse, before we make further application of our discourse to the present occasion.

All these died in (or according to) *faith*

The Apostle in this Epistle had most sweetly opened the doctrine of Christ to the Hebrews that were partakers of the heavenly call, and thereby brought to beleeve, and thence called holy brethren (*ch.*3.1.) and from his natures, offices, sufferings, and from the dignity of them all, he had abundantly evinced and cleared it, that they had good ground to hold fast the faith and profession of him firm without wavering, and not be moved therefrom by any cause or reason: In the 10th Chapter he had laid down many other arguments also to presse them thereunto, as from the danger of willing backsliding, *If we sin willfully, after the knowledge of the truth, there remains no more sacrifice for sin,* &c. verf.25,26. and from the consideration of the excellency apprehended by them in Christ in their illumination, and the effects of that apprehension in them, &c. verf.
33,34.

33.34. *Remember the daies in which after ye Were illuminated, ye endured a great fight of affliction,* &c. from the greatnesse of the reward promised, and to be certainly enjoied by them in its season, if they hold fast their faith and confidence, and were not turned aside therefrom. *verf.*35. *Cast not away your confidence Which hath great recompence of reward,* to which he adds an instruction about their need of patience, *ver.*36. and usefullnesse and excellency of faith, as that which most suiteth with the condition in which God useth to leade his, and in which they should meet with preservation unto the enjoyment of the reward promised them, *verf.* 38. *Now the just shall live by faith,* or, the just by faith shall live: without that the profession will be worthlesse, the confidence will vanish, and patience will have no place: but there will either be an open revolting or a secret withdrawing in a barren, empty, dead adhering to an outside profession. Now in this Chapter he confirms what he had there said, that faith is that in which God exerciseth his people, and gives them life, that God doth not use to keep them by sense, in giving in an enjoyment of things promised, so much as by faith in his word without sensible feelings and experiments: but first of all, he laies down a definition of this faith, *v.* 3. Its the subsistance of things hoped for, and the evidence or argument of things not seen, that puts an end to vain empty disputations, How do you know that God made the world, or that the Scriptures are the word of God, or are true &c? Faith makes it evident to me. God hath said thus, and in his saying I am convinced and perswaded to believe, though I see not the things of which he speaketh to me, and in believing I am staied and satisfied about it, and its become to me as firm a principle as if I had seen. Its an argument leaning upon Gods authority, speaking and manifesting it self unto the conscience, that gives a subsistence to things hoped for, as to my minde: so that though we see not the things we hope for, nor are they as yet in being, yet they being beleeved, have a kinde of subsistence in the heart: and the soul acteth upon that subsistence towards them as really as if it sawthem with the bodily sense, as if they were already existent and had a being, which also they shall have in their season. From that the Apostle proceeds to give divers instances of the excellency, usefullnesse and efficacy of this faith in the prime and choice Saints of God in all ages, how they have lived by it, and in the exercise of it, without the enjoyment of the things set before them and beleeved: and he begins at Abel, v. 4. and so passes on to *Enoch,* ver. 5 *Noah,* ver. 7 and thence to *Abraham,* *Isaac,* and *Jacob,* ver. 8, 9. and *Sarah,* ver. 11. or whom he here

saith

faith in the text, *All these died in faith, not having received the promises,* &c.

The words (*these all*) seem to referre to *Abraham, Isaac, Jacob* and *Sarah,* both because of *Enoch,* of whom its said *verf.5.* that he was translated that he should not see death, who therefore cannot be here included (except we take his change in his translation to be equivalent to death) and also because that he tels us *verf.15,* of these forsaking their Countrey, which we finde no where affirmed of those others mentioned before these. But let us come to the words, and note something from them, that present themselves unto us, for I shall not spend time about a curious superfluous cutting them in pieces: *Abraham, Isaac* and *Jacob* were worthy persons highly favoured of God, chosen by him to peculiar dignity and priviledges, Princes and Prophets, and very famous in their proper seasons, yet behold what the Apostle in the first words of the text affirmeth of them all, *These all died,* Whence let us note (and I shall but briefly note things, and not bound up my discourse unto the unfolding of some one only proposition)

Note 1.

That no dignity or priviledge though very great will exempt us from dying.

Death is a due debt to nature, *Omne quod generatur corrumpitur,* whatsoever hath a naturall generation is also subject to corruption, death is in the present principles of every earthly living being, and that as by mans sinne meritoriously, so by Gods just sentence upon mans sinning judicially, *Statutum est,* &c. *Its enacted,* resolved upon and ordained *for man once to die,* and that *once,* though for *time* uncertain to us, yet that it shall finde a *time,* nothing more sure, yea, many a time it seems very near us, and we are in a tendency to it from our birth to our last gasp. By many waies, diseases, infirmities or providentiall accidents we may, and by some or other of them we are sure to arrive at death: we reade of none exempted save *Enoch* and *Elias,* the first changed, the other assumed (for as for the Virgin *Mary* we have not such authentick authority or warrant to beleeve it) those two did God exempt from the common way of flesh, to shew in them his power over all flesh, over nature and naturall principles and inclinations, and that we might the more readily be induced to believe the benefit of Christ in the resurrection of the dead, when we hear that he preserved some from death and made them as pledges to us of the certainty of that glory and immortality that is the promised portion of all that believe in him through his death. And yet surely even they underwent a change equivalent to death, though

Heb.9,27.

they

they slept not in death, as the Apostle saies, 1 *Cor.* 15.51. *We shall not all sleep, but we shall all be changed*, though we lie not in death, yet we must passe through it, we must put off this mortality, these innate principles of death: we shall not be as now we are, when we come to inherit what now we believe for. But for us and the rest of mankinde death in a more proper way is to be expected by us, and will come upon us (except the coming of Christ should suddenly prevent us, and then such a change might be allotted us) It's not the being great or gracious that exempts from that event, *These all died*, many have lived many years, yet (as the longest day hath its night) so this hath been the constant Catastrophe and winding up of them all in their genealogies, *They all died: Jared* lived nine hundred and sixty two years, and then he died : *Methuselah* lived nine hundred sixty and nine years, but then it follows too, he also died : so *Noah* and *Abraham* and *Isaac* and *Jacob*, all gracious and holy men, and found righteous in the . generations, and yet these all died. It's that that *David* propounds to all, *Psa* 49.1,2. *high and low, rich and poor, one and other*, because its the lot of all, that death will o-vertake them all, none can shift from it, *None can give a ransome to God for his brother, that he should live alwaies and never die, the price is too great and it ceaseth for ever.* We see wise men die as well as fools, righteous men as well as sinners, Magistrates as well as Subjects, rich as well as poor, one as well as another, there is no escape of any in this battel, nay men as well as the bruit beasts, for as to this common condition of flesh, there is one event to them both, though not as to the spirits of both, nor as to the supernaturall work of the re-surrection of the body, but as to death, one thing happeneth to both, both are of the dust, and both go to the dust: *Not only they but we al-so must needs all die, and our strength is as Water spilt upon the ground, neither is there any respect of persons with God.* Serius aut citius, &c. sooner or later we must all stoop to death in the flesh, *These all died.*

A truth known to all, and to be experimented by us all, and yet a truth as little thought of as almost any, and as little made use of, well might *David* cry out as he did, when he was about to speak thereof *Audite hoc omnes populi*, &c. *Psal.*49.1.Hear this all ye peo-ple, for though we all see it, and shall feel it, yet we minde it not, few incline their ears to hear what God saies to us in it, but hear this all ye people, rich and poor, high and low, one and other, All must die : Ye that are rich and wealthy, and have scraped much together, and laid it up for posterity, ye must die, and leave all this that ye have gotten, and ye know not who shall possesse it after you. Hear this all

B   ye

ye gallants of the world that are fine and fashionable, and delight
to deck up your selves in costly apparell, *Quid im colitis escam ver-*
mibus? you must die and leave these bodies which you so dresse up,
for the worms to feed upon. Hear this ye that addict your selves
to pleasures, and rejoice in a thing of nought, and make your selves
merry with meer vanities, ye must all die, and death will put an end
to your mirth and jollity, to your pleasure and voluptuousnesse,
chambering and wantonnesse, and nothing but the guilt of these
things shall descend with you. Hear this ye that are poor and pincht
with want, and bitten with sorrow, that fill your selves with cares,
and pine away with grief, ye must die too, and then your poverty
and afflictions here shall have an end, ye shall then have no more
need of what now ye murmure, or grieve, or turmoil your selves for
want of: It's but a momentany condition that you are here afflicted
with, ye must die, and death will put an end to it, yea, death will put
an end to all these things, weal and woe, sorrow and mirth, riches
and pleasures, and whatever here we have, as to us. *Surely man in*
Psal. 39.6.   *his best estate here is altogether vanity,* like a bubble full of winde and
emptinesse, easily broken and blown away with a blast, and then that
that was sweld up into a great appearing magnitude, proves as nothing, makes no further shew or appearance that we should look
after it; Oh! why then do ye pursue after vain things? why sport
ye your selves so eagerly in voluptuousnesse? or spend so much cost
on dust and ashes, and pride your selves of that ye have no hold on?
or care so much for that that strangers or victors may devour up
when you are gone? why labour ye for that that perisheth, and delight in that that will not endure? Sure the very thought of death
might instruct us all to sobriety in all conditions: Sobriety in earthly
delights, for we must leave them, Sobriety in honours and prefer-
ments, for we must leave them, Sobriety in apparell, for we must
leave it, Sobriety in caring for and getting in the things of this
1 Tim. 6.7.   world, for we must leave them: *As we brought nothing into the*
World with us, so we are sure we can carry nothing out with us, Sobriety in all things for we must die to them, Sobriety in fears of grow-
Psal. 49.17, 18.   ing enemies, *Be not thou afraid when one is made rich, and the glory of*
his house is encreased, yea, though he be one that hates thee, and so
hath more power visibly to harm thee, *for his day will come,* he also
is but mortall, and death will overtake him, and bring down his excellency, and *when he dies, he shall not take any thing with him, nor*
Isa. 57.13.   *shall his glory and pomp descend after him;* who art thou that thou shoul-
dest be afraid of a man that shall die, and of the Son of man that shall be

made as graffe? though here enemies be strong and potent, and use their power wickedly to persecute the innocent and oppresse them, yet this their state is but for a moment, they also shall die and goe down to the dust, and then *where is their fury?* in the grave we shall be quiet, and they have no power to harm us: *There the wicked cease* from troubling, and there the weary are at rest, there the prisoners rest together, and they hear not the voice of the oppressour, the small and great are there, and the servant is free from his master,* yea, the thought of death might further us in taking of our Saviours counsell, *Joh.6. 29. Labour not for the meat that perisheth, but for that that will endure to life eternall.* Set not we our hearts on these things, whereof death will surely deprive us, and we know not how near that is unto us: but look we after those things that will abide with us after death, and carry us through death, which it hath no power over, nor can take from us, the favour of God, the light of his countenance, faith and a good conscience, assurance of eternal happinesse, when thou hast these things thou must rejoice indeed: and thy joy. nor men, nor death can take away from thee, *These all died.*

But wherefore died they? There might be many reasons given, but I will not insist upon them, they died that they might be removed from the evil of the world, and not alwaies therewith burthened, *Isa.57 1. The righteous is taken away from the evil to come,* and *they died that they might rest from their labour,* Rev. 14.13. that having done their work and served their generation (as is said of *David*, Act.13.36.) they might goe to bed and sleep, they shall enter into rest or peace: *they shall rest in their beds, each one walking in his uprightnesse,* Isa.57.2. thence death is usually in Scripture called a sleep, such a one fell asleep, and such a one slept with his fathers: thence the heathen Poets have also called sleep *Placidissima mortis imago,* and τῦ θανάτῦ ἡς προμελέτησι, the pleasant image, resemblance, and as it were the premeditation of death. But I passe from these things, and goe forward with the text, for this is not the businesse that the Apostle here mainly propounds, though very usefull for us to consider, and at this time also very seasonable and sutable with our present occasion, that we also might be stirred up with earnestnesse to pray as that good man of God, *Psa.90.12. So teach us O Lord to number our daies, that we may apply our hearts unto wisedome:* but the Apostle adds,

These all died (κατὰ πίστιν) in (or according to) *faith, Secundum fidem,* after the faith. What? Did they die in faith? Did their faith die? Verily no, they did not cast away their faith when they died,

but

but exercised it : their act of dying too was done in faith, and according to their faith, they died in an exercise of faith, that it might be further manifest (according to the first proposition and prime intent of the Apostle here) that they did live by faith, as they did believe in God while they lived, so when they came to die, they yeelded up themselves to God in that belief, and were not shaken from it, no not by death : they feared not in the valley of the shadow of death, *Psa* 23 3. nor fainted in the hour of death, *Gen.* 49.18. even then also they waited for Gods salvation, though death ceised on their bodies, yet they retained, and let not goe their confidence : though the day of their lives here was expired, yet died not their hopes and hearts within them, but were supported by faith, with the expectation of another day, in which the promises should be enjoyed, and here we may further note the excellency of faith.

They that live by faith die in faith, the just by faith side life through their faith, even in the midst of death.

These all died in faith, In this these righteous ones differ from others, All die, but die not κατα πιςιν, as becometh faith, or with an experiment of the power of faith, all die passively, they suffer the pains of death, and have their lives fetched from them, but all are not active in death, willingly and believingly to resign up their spirits to God, and cast themselves into his arms with confidence that he will keep and restore them, and notwithstanding death intervene their receit of his word and the performance of his promise, yet he will not fail of his word, but perform every jot and tittle of it to them. This is the carriage and priviledge of those that have the word of God abiding in and united by faith with them, *These all died in faith,* these die in the Lord, 1 *Th.*4.16.*Rev.*14.3. Through faith they close with and are enclosed in the power, strength and vertue of the Lord Jesus Christ, by which their souls are acted and carried with lively hope and expectation of good from God through him, and as they live in him so they die in him too, as they walk in his vertue and power while alive in the body, so in the same vertue & power putting forth it self in (yea encompassing) their souls, through faith they depart out of the body unto God, and depose themselves with God, till the time in which he shall restore them. These hold fast their faith to the death and in death, that they might be examples and encouragements to us also to hold it fast, that we may have the like use and benefit of it in our deaths. But may some object.

Object.

But how do these things stand together, Faith and Death ? When Christ hath said, that if a man keep his saying he shall never see death,

death ? *Joh.* 8.51. What is it to keep his saying but to believe his sayings, and hold fast that belief ? and did not *Abraham* keep his sayings, and the Prophets keep his sayings, might not we be offended at Chrift as the Jews were, and fay with them, All thefe had faith, and kept it to the death, and yet as the Apoftle here witneffeth, they all notwithstanding that, died, how is it then that Chrift faith, If any man keep my sayings he fhall never fee death ?

Anfw.

Oh how mysterious is the word of God, and what a riddle to flefhly wisedom and humane fenfe ! It's to be believed and held for true by faith, not to be judged of as true or falfe by the verdict of our fenfe: certainly both Chrift and his Apoftles faid the truth, he that keeps his sayings fhall not fee death, and yet thefe that kept his sayings (for before *Abraham* was Chrift was, and his sayings they were that he received) did all die, yea, the Apoftle here hints a folution to that doubt of the appearing contradiction in them, when he faies *thefe all died in faith,* for in this very thing that they died in faith, they were fo preferved that they did not fee death, for this very faith in which they died, carried them above fenfe, and took their eye off from death, and fet it upon life, fo that they faw, found felt, experimented life in death, even when they died according to the flefh, yet they even lived in their spirits ; their bodies did but fleep in death, while their spirits lived above death, being made partakers of Jefus Chrift (as he word of God to be made flefh, who is the refurrection and the life) and the very death of death, putting it to death, they paffed through the fhadow of it, but they faw not, felt not, found not the fubftance of it, they faw God in their death, and the fight of him fo took up and filled their eye that they could not fee death Or 2. they faw not that death that is *ôis ôiôra*, for ever, for indeed that is death and worthy the name of death, *the fecond death,* the other, the firft death, the condemnation that came by the firft man upon all men, that fpent it felf upon Chrift, being by the wife and merciful God that flated upon him, and he hath abolifhed it fo in and by himfelf, that nothing but the carcaffe and fhadow of it abideth for us to fee or grapple with, fo that he that fees but it, fees not death properly but only the fhadow and fhell of it : Its life, power, and proper vigour is by the death of Chrift fwallowed up, abolifhed and gone; he then that never fees the fecond death, fees not death, for there is no other death by way of punifhment of man for his finne, that's properly death, but it, remaining, and that hath no power upon Chrift or any in him: the juft fhall live by faith in the midft of the fhadow of the other death, and he fhall live out

Rom 3.12,

2 Tim. 1.10

of

of the way and danger of this second death, he shall never be hurt of it either by the bearing it or fearing it, his faith shall keep him from the first, and being exercised carry him through and above the second, and he shall never be overcome or over-powred by it, *thence blessed and holy is he that hath part in the first resurrection,* that hath part in Christ the first begotten from the dead, the resurrection and the life, that in their spirits are raised with him, and shall have their bodies raised with the just at his glorious appearing.

Seeing then that we must all needs die, and that's our portion in the flesh, and there is a way by which we may so die as not to see death, *viz.* to die in faith, what wisdom is it to take that course that we may so die, that we may see no death when we die, feel no sting in death, finde it but a shadow that hath no deadly substance in it, nay rather finde it lighted with the glory of eternall life, seen and tasted through it? that we may see life in death, a life beyond, above and without death. Oh how terrible is death to men when they see death in it! when they experiment and feel a sting in it, the sting of a self-condemning conscience, and the pricks of the second death in the first death. When they see death and nothing but death, when life is hid from their eyes, and so their hearts and thoughts die within them together with or before their bodies: when they die full of despair, strangers from and hopelesse of ever finding the life of God: that will be a black griesly day to a soul that sees not life in it, what need then to cry to God here, *so to teach us to number our daies, that We may apply our hearts to Wisedom?* the wisedom of God in its sayings, reproofs, counsels, cals, that it powring out its spirit upon us, and opening its precious words to us, we may be filled with faith and courage, and be in such a state as in which to see no death, that we may so believe and live in and by faith in the power and exercise of it, that in all our dying conditions, yea, when we come to breath out our souls we may die in faith, die according to faith and not according to sense; Even some believers not living and dying in an exercise of faith, are many times filled with sorrow, fears, faintings, especially in their dying cases, because they judge not, and so die not according to faith, they judge according to sense, they feeling pain and feeling temptations, and seeing griesly things represented to them by Satan, they are affrighted and terrified at them, though they be false illusions, whereas exercising faith, and so judging according to it, they are carried above, and get the victory over sense and temptation. Let us therefore so follow on after wisedom, that her words may dwell richly in us,

that

that her spirit may be a spirit of faith in us, that we may live in faith, and have a living exercise of faith in all conditions, so shall we also dying have our hearts born up by faith, and shall be enabled to lay down our tabernacle with peace and joy, as that will leade us, and not with trouble, as sense would carry us, and unbelief affright us, while we judge of God and Christ, life and death, sinne and righteousnesse according to faith, and not according to carnall sense and philosophicall speculations, we shall be from seeing death when we die, yea, shall finde and feel life in the shadow of death, according to that *Joh.* 5.24. *He that heareth my Word, and believeth on him that sent me hath eternall life,* and shall not come into judgement, but is passed from death to life, and that *Joh,* 11.25,26. *I am the resurrection and the life, he that believeth in me, though he were dead, yet shall he live, and he that liveth and believeth, shall never die.*

These all died in faith.

Faith? Ay, but what is faith, and how may a man come by it?   *Object.*

The Apostle in this Chapter *Heb.* 11.1. tels us what it is: It's ἔλεγχ⍵ (or as the paraphrase hath it ἀπόδειξις) τῶν μὴ βλεπομένων *the argument and demonstration of things not seen,* of invisible things that are not the objects of sense, but that are declared in the word of God: such is the vertue and power of faith, that it gives as great a certainty of those unseen things to the soul or minde, as can be made over by any scientificall demonstration, for so ἔλεγχ⍵ signifies, a demonstration to the minde, not a presentation to the bodily essence, as the Greek Scholiast upon it, ἀποδείκνυσι ὁρατὰ τὰ ἀόρατα: ἡ πίστις πᾶς τῶν κ. τὰ ἱς ἐλπίσι &c. Faith presents invisible things as visible: how? to the minde and hope: which hope also springeth from it, and is upheld by it, as it there follows, it's ὑπόστασις τῶν ἐλπιζομένων too, *the basis or subsistence of things hoped for,* It so presents divine things to the minde, that it also draws in the soul to trust in God, and hope for good from him, and the good things it hopes for, faith gives bottom to, and enables the soul to act towards them, as if they had a reall existence as was before noted. And for the way to come by this faith, the Apostle tels us *Fides ex auditu,* &c. *Faith is by hearing,* by that means God effecteth it, whence that in *Isa.* 55.3. *Hear, and your souls shall live.* Ay, but it's not every hearing that produces this faith, but that which is by the word of God, the hearing of the Gospel or word of faith that's both mother and nurse of it, from that it springs, and by that it's nourished: in listening to that God puts forth his mighty arm, and enables the soul to believe, as sometimes

                                    Rom. 10.17

times

times he did to the Ifraelites by the brazen Serpent, and to *Naaman* in the waters of *Jordan* to heal them, *He that hears my words and believes on him that sent me*, &c. *Joh* 5.24. Hearing the Word is the way to believe in God.

First, God declareth the truth, which is truth when declared by him, not made truth by our believing : this truth heard perfwades the foul by the divine power and fpirit, which is therewith miniftred, to clofe with what it hears, and clofing with what it hears, the fame power and fpirit doth therethrough further (while therein are o-pened excellent things, as the hatred and juftice of God againft fin, and yet his love, mercy and good will in Chrift toward the finfull foul, &c.) perfwade the foul to embrace and clofe with Chrift him-felf, of whom the truth witneffeth, and unto whom as its proper body and fountain (as God is in him and he is God) it leadeth, and fo the foul is by the Word heard, and through the divine power of God therein, brought unto Chrift, and in and through Chrift un-to God, by the beam to the body of the Sun, and in that to all that fountain, fullneffe of glorious light that fils that body, and makes it fo glorious.

But indeed the nature of this faith in which thefe holy men of God died, and which is of fo glorious ufe in life and death, is in the text it felf by its Acts and operations notably laid forth and defcri-bed. I fhall briefly and but briefly touch upon them : *Thefe all died in faith not having received the promifes*, faith ftands not in mens ha-ving in poffeffion or actuall fruition the things promifed, for then faith and fenfe fhould be confounded, but 1. they fee them (*the pro-mifes*) afar off,

That's the firft act of this faith, though alone of it felf it is not faith, for it's faid of fome *they have feen and hated* Joh.15.24. yet this is I fay, the firft act of this faith, or the firft act tending to this faith, through which thefollowing acts are alfo generated where this is rightly feated, and the abiding in this and of this, is that in and through which the other acts are carried on too and perpetuated : this act being the firft product of the Word heard, and that which moft immediatly fpringeth from it : for while God fpeaketh, he prefents in his fpeakings truth to the foul, and the foul hearing and receiving in the word fpoken, findes therein and therewith a divine power illuminating and giving light to it, and power of difcerning that light, as if the light of the Sun coming to a blinde man in a dungeon, fhould both prefent light to him, and in the fame moment give him a faculty and power of feeing : thus in *Pfa.*139.130. the entrance of thy Word giveth light, and giveth understanding to the simple; the soul receiving or looking upon divine word sees things set before it, that it never so saw before, as his own vileneffe and filthineffe, and Gods goodneffe and compaffions, and the great and glorious things in his way (his Son) to be met with and enjoied. But these are said to have seen them afarre of, πόῤῥωθεν. God shews the end from the beginning : things to be done never so long time hence, yet being revealed in the word and there presented, are by faith seen ; indeed men not hearkning to the word, miffe of much light and knowledge therein held forth, and see not many things which in wist viewing or diligent attention they might come to see, things afar off, the things promised, which were not of a long time to be performed, whence neither had they so full and clear a sight of them as those that see them in nearer times, as things seen afar off at a great diftance are not so fully and clearly seen, as when they are seen nearer hand. Now they are brought near to us, these being the laft times, yea, some of these promises that they saw through the word at a diftance are already in part performed, and are become Gofpel declarations to us, as the coming and resurrection of Chrift, of the former whereof *Mary* could in her time say (much more may we now) *He hath holpen his servant Israel in remembrance of his mercy as he spake to our forefathers, to Abraham and to his seed for ever,* Luk. 1. 25. And the Apoftle *Paul* declares the latter as another ftep of the performance of these promises, saying, *We declare unto you good tidings, how that the promise that was made unto the fathers God hath fullfilled the same unto us their children, in that he hath raised up Jesus from the dead.* We believing see them by faith as things already done, and they are the grounds of our believing in him for those further things contained in those promises, which are yet unfullfilled, and which we are to expect the performance of in his feafon, but then there muft be with this seeing a further act, even that that follows in the next place of them, *viz.*

2. They were perfwaded.

That's the second act in this divine faith, it's not a bare speculation of truths in the propofition without a perfwafion, that they are truths, and worthy to be heeded and embraced by them, the difcerning of divine truths as propounded is a means to perfwafion, and so to believing (Joh. 6. 40. *Every one that sees the Son, and believes on him, &c.)* and is it self augmented, and flows in more upon the soul through believing, but is not it self faith without perfwafion, nor can it be so called : these worthies in their faith saw and were perfwaded they were not ἀπειθεῖς or ὑιοὶ ἀπειθείας Children of unperfwafiblenefs, difobedient

Isa. 46. 10.

to the heavenly vifion, like men that fee things at a diftance prefented to them, but yet cannot be perfwaded they are indeed the things they feem to be, becaufe they know not how or which way fuch things fhould come there, and they muft have their reafon fatisfied in that, or elfe they will think it's an illufion and ftrong mifapprehenfion in their fenfes. No it is not fo with faith, though they faw but afarre off, yet they were perfwaded of the truth and certainty of what was fhewed them, and of what in that fhewing they did fee : In which they differed from many that now though they have the Gofpel more nearly, clearly and plainly prefenting the things of God to them, yet they are not perfwaded of them, they fee fuch things affirmed, but cannot think they are fo as they feem to be affirmed of ; they exalt their reafon, and cannot deny themfelves, and be willing to become fools to follow the word of God, and to come to its fayings, they have many queftions naufeoufly lie upon their ftomacks through the exercife of their flefhly wifedom, of which they are fick, and in which they muft be fore-fatisfied, or elfe they cannot be perfwaded: like *Nicodemus,* How can this and that be ? *Can a man enter into his mothers womb again, and be born a fecond time ?* or like old *Zachary, how can perfons fo ftricken in years have the promife of a childe made good unto them ?* or thofe in the wilderneffe, *Can God prepare a table ?* &c. But fo it is not with faith, it faies not, *Who fhall afcend up into heaven to fetch down Chrift ?* or *Who fhall defcend into the deep to bring him up ?* it raifes not up queftions, it ftumbles not through its reafonings, but is perfwaded through the confideration of Gods authority, *They were perfwaded,* and yet it refts not there neither, but as it follows of thefe holy ones

Rom. 10, 6, 7.

3. They embraced them.

Και ασπασαμενοι and faluting or kiffing them: ay, this is the completive, intrinfecall act of faith, the faith which the juft do live by. It's not a bare fight and perfwafion, but fuch as in which the heart liketh, and clofeth with the things prefented, and whereof they are perfwaded. It's poffible a man may fee and be perfwaded of truth, and yet not like but hate it, not falute and embrace it, but turn his back upon it and reject it : fome were perfwaded *that Chrift was the heir,* yet were fo far from embracing him, that they added, *Come, let us kill him :* even fo many a man when he fees a truth which reproves his way, and is not for his turn, his luft, purpofe or defign, though he fee and be perfwaded it's true, yet his heart loves it not, but boggles againft it, he cannot like to entertain it, the young man that came to Chrift *Mat.* 19.22, could not nor did object againft Chrifts doctrine, nay, it feems he was in fome meafure perfwaded it was true, why elfe fhould it have troubled him,

Mat. 21. 38.

and

and made him sad? had he given no credit to it, it would never have come so near his heart, he would lightlier have got rid of it, but yet he could not embrace or welcome it, though there was a precious promise set before him, yet he could not like it upon those terms on which it was propounded: it was not his case alone, many could like to have the happinesse promised in the Gospel, and are perswaded that upon such and such terms they might and should have it, who yet not liking those terms do not embrace it, like *Boaz* his kinsman, he could like to have redeemed *Naomies* lands, till he came to see the terms, that it would spoil his own inheritance, and upon these terms he would none of it: many would own and embrace truth, were it not that it would spoil them of their self-interests, if it leade them not to such self-deniall. But this divine faith here spoken of carries the heart above those stumbles, and makes it with chearfullnesse and joy to welcome the glorious grace and promised portion that truth presents it upon its own terms: It so acts the will and affections too, that they like what the soul sees in truth, and is perswaded of, and take it home, and give it the best entertainment they possibly can, it unites the soul unto the promise, and the promise findes a subsistence in the soul: It's as a match that God hath propounded, and the soul accepts it upon Gods terms, owns, loves, sides with and rejoices in it: upon which follows,

4. They confessed themselves strangers and pilgrims in the earth, thereby declaring plainly that they seek a countrey.

Here we have faith compleated inwardly in its own essence, further perfecting it self in its fruit and operation, as the tree may be said to be perfected in its bearing fruit: Here's an inward hope and expectation of the thing promised, and in that a seeking after it, *a countrey*, another and a better state, *a new heaven and a new earth*, that's the ultimate thing promised, *the state of restauration of all things*, and therein the full enjoyment of God: now through faith (that is through the word of promise, seen, perswaded of and embraced) they are *begot to a living hope*, and that puts the soul upon pressing after the glory promised, and purges the soul from the earthly affections, that fill the hearts of those that have not so beleeved: all they had before were now nothing to what they see and were perswaded of and embraced. These promises or things promised are so welcome to their souls though yet they possesse them not, but only have the faith of them, that earth and world and all things here are not to be compared with them, they reckon themselves not at home till they enjoy them, their mindes are after them, and off from these things that they lived upon, before these better things were revealed to them: Here's mortificati-

on

on effected both in minde and conversation, the affections removed from the things below, and set upon these things that are above, taken off from present enjoyment and advantages for enjoying the world, and set upon the promised future happinesse, the heart is taken and gone after another city and countrey, and that heart-belief and inward affection, produces mouth and practice-confession to salvation, they confessed themselves strangers and pilgrims in this earth, they finde not herein a resting place, they have a better home, and that they seek after, I know others may utter such like words upon other principles, as men seeing the brevity and uncertainty of mans life, may think they have here no staying continuance, as *Cicero* the heathen Philosopher speaks somewhat to that purpose, *I go* (saith he) *out of this life, as if I went out of an Inne, not out of my dwelling-house, for nature hath given us here a place to bait in only, not to dwell in.* Thus a morall man may be led to say by the sense and knowledge he hath of this lifes uncertainty and passing swiftnesse, but their confession proceeded from their faith in an earnest seeking after Gods heavenly promises : the belief of Gods word, and the complacency they had therein in the expectation of the things set before them, made them so to reckon themselves as strangers and pilgrims in the earth, and therefore not to love or covet after the enjoiments of the earth, not to minde to return back into their own countrey, whence by faith they had departed to follow after God : all see they cannot here alwaies continue, but all know not that they have a better countrey : and therefore all that so see are not mortified in their mindes to the things whose vanity they see : all reckon not (nor so walk as if they reckoned) themselves strangers and pilgrims in the earth seeking another countrey.

Two things we may principally note from what hath been said here about the nature of faith and efficacy thereof.

Note 3, 1. *That that divine faith that will indeed do us good in death stands in the word of God, the word of the promise or Gospel, closes with and springs from that, sees, is perswaded of and embraces the testimony of God held forth in that.*

Note 4. 2. *That that divine faith is exceeding operative and working inwardly and outwardly, embracing the heavenly things propounded, it leads to look for, expect and seek them, and to despise these earthly things, in comparison*

Tit. 2 11,12. *of them. It leads to deny ungodlinesse and worldly lusts, and to live soberly, righteously and godly in this present world, looking for the blessed hope, the promised inheritance at the appearance of Christ Jesus.* It's neither a groundlesse humane conception and presumption, nor an empty, barren and idle speculation, It's such an heart-closing with the word

Ex hâc vitâ ita discedo tanquam ex hospitio, non tanquam ex domo, commorandi enim diversorium natura nobis, non habitandi dedit.

as in which the word is vigorous in the heart, and brings forth fruit unto eternal life: this in both parts we have seen already, in the opening of the text, they saw them afar off and were perswaded, and embracing them confessed that they were but strangers and pilgrims in the earth.

Would we have faith, or would we that have any measure of it grow therein? let us take heed to the word, the word of faith, the doctrine of the Gospel, and let us be swift to hear, slow to speak, or make confessions or protestations of our faith further then that heard effecteth them in us: be more ready to hear what God saies to us, then to boast our selves of what is in us, or to offer the sacrifice of fools, such as the power of the truths we hear spring not up in us: much more be we slow to speak against the Gospel of God, because we comprehend it not with our reason, or to be wroth and offended thereat because it comes to lay us low, and pull down our proud swelling conceptions. Hearken diligently, and your souls shall live. *Applic.*

Eccl. 5, 1.

Isa. 55. 3.

And so, would we be means to bring others to faith? preach we and hold we forth the word to them, not our dictates and placitas, but Gods word, the Gospel as attested in the Scripture, that men may believe as the Scripture hath said, for to such faith is the promise made, *Joh. 9. 38. He that believeth on me, as the Scripture hath said, out of his belly shall flow rivers of living water*, and for such believers Christ hath praied, *Joh. 17. 20. for them that shall believe through their word*, the word given by Christ to his Apostles whom he sent out into the world: preach the word of promise, for of that it is that the heirs are born that shall enjoy the inheritance, the word of the death and of the resurrection of Jesus Christ for men, which is part of the promise made to *Abraham*, as was shewed before, that's the foundation doctrine: upon this foundation build them, and then exhort them to walk worthy thereof in all well-pleasing. There's many a mans faith detect'd to be vain by these two things; by its want of a right bottom, and by its want of right fruits and operations. 1. Thou saist thou believest and trustest in God, but according to what dost thou believe? it's with many a man because of and according to their works, diligence, endeavours, sense, feelings, not according as it is said in the word to us (as it's said of *Abraham, he believed according to what was spoken to him, So shall thy seed be*, Ro. 4. 17.) Now as that's not right faith that carries not on the soul after God, and causes it not to seek the countrey promised, so neither is that right faith that springs from mans own strifts and endeavours after the love of God, as that's not a good faith that's without works, so neither is that good that's bottomed upon thy works. It's the character of true beleevers in *Act.* 18. 27. *that they*

Joh. 17. 10. Gal. 4. 23.

beleeved

beleeved through grace, not through works, I believe saies one, that Chrift died for me, and is a Mediatour for me. Well but how cameft thou by that faith ? whereupon is it grounded ? why they will fay perhaps from the word: Well, let us fee how the word evidenced it tothee? why, I found fuch and fuch effects wrought in me, I was convinced of my evil way, and humbled, and mourned, and reformed, and was thus and thus changed, therefore I perceived that I was one of the elect of God, and Chrift died for me. Oh but now believeft thou not according to the word but deceiveft thy felf, grounding thy faith of Chrifts mediation upon thy works, or the effects of law and confcience in thee, &c. I fear when thou comeft to the triall, thy works will be found light and vain. What doft thou tell me of fruits and effects of faith, evidencing thine election before, and as the ground of thy believing Chrift a Mediatour for thee ? No changes or fruits will evidence election, but fuch fpring from faith in Chrift in whom the election is, nor is there any faith rightly in Chrift as now come, but in his bloud and mediation, *Rom.3.25. by his bloud we have acceffe to God,* to believe in him, and approach to him, and fee his love to us : and canft thou have faith in his bloud before thou knoweft whether he fhed any for thee, that thereby thou mighteft know he fhed it for thee ? faith in the bloud of Chrift is this, through the knowledge and belief of his bloud fhed, to be imboldned to approach to and rely on God, and expect good from him as from one that thereby hath teftified his good will toward thee, and opened a way of acceffe to himfelf and to his Kingdome for thee, that thou mighteft come to him, and hope in him for it. It's ftrange that Chrifts bloud fhould give thee boldneffe to rely on God, when thou knoweft not whether ever it was fhed for thee, or that thou hadft any thing to do with it : thou fayft it was fhed for all that believe, and thou believeft, &c. That it was fhed for all that believe, is not queftioned, but that very believing is to be in that bloud: Now the doubt is of thy believing in it, before thou feeft Gods word hold it forth as fhed for thee, that fo thou mighteft know it's fhed for thee: I fay that believing of thine was not a right believing in it, that preceded thy belief of it by divine teftimony to be fhed for thee : It was fhed for enemies and ungodly, that being preached to them they might believe in it, as well as for them as believing in it, that they might be fanctified and faved by it. If thou believeft in it or thinkeft to have falvation by it, becaufe of thy former felf-actings to forrow and to reformation, then is not this faith right, becaufe not fpringing from the word, yea, thou inverteft the order of the Apoftle, he tels us they were faved from their filthineffe and difobedience, and led to deny ungodlineffe and worldly

Tit. 2. 11, 12,
& 3. 4, 5.

lnfts

lusts by the grace, the love and pity of God to man appearing, and thou first art led to reform and alter and deny thy lusts, and to believe as thou thinkest before thou apprehendest his grace, and then drawest an inference of his grace from those thy works and denials, thou endeavourest and conceitest thy self to work well, and thereupon buildest an opinion that God loved thee, and Christ came and died for thee, this faith springs from thy works and not from the word, the testimony of God is not believed by thee. Oh but thou wilt say, Even all those frames were begotten by the grace of God in thee, else thou couldest not have had them, and it was in hearing his word that thou wast led to them. Ay, but what meanest thou by grace? the good will of God in Christ fore-manifested to thee in the word of the Gospel? No, for that thou sawest not, but fetchest in by consequence upon thy changes : what then ? a certain secret insensible working of power in thy heart to perswade thee to confesse thy sins, and mend thy actions, and do better then formerly? Now thou speakest in the dialect of that Pharisee, *Luk* 18.10,11. He had such a like considence that he was a righteous, justified person, and was in state of grace : but how came he by it ? he trusted in himself, he saies not to be made righteous, but that he was now a righteous one, one that should have benefit by the Messias in his coming, and should partake of the promises, he fetched the arguments of his confidence from himself, and yet what he speaks of as in him he attributes to Gods grace as if he had wrought it in him, God I thank thee that I am not thus and thus, he doth not ascribe it to himself but to God, and it's not likely but he thought God had perswaded him so and so to walk by what he had heard of his will in the Scriptures, in the law of God, he thought of a secret working of power in the word, but he never apprehended or believed the grace, that is, the good will of God, as it was preach d to *Abraham* in the Gospel and promise, he was *ignorant of Gods righteousnesse*, he was *born of the bond-woman*, his changes and righteousnesse sprang not from love and grace fore-apprehended, but from the Law enjoyning and adding promises to mans observation, and therefore this plea would no serve him, his confidence was not currant, nor did God accept him. Such is thy profession, thou findest it said, *If thou believest thou shalt be saved* which (in it self only considered) is but like a legall promise, and nothing differs from it, for that saies, if thou dost thus and thus, thou shalt live or be saved ; but herein the Gospel differs from it, that it laies down a foundation of love demonstrated from God to a sinner, in the first place to move him, impower and enable him to the thing required of him: so doth not the law, but only holds forth a conditionall

1 Cor.10.13. Gal.4.23,24.

nall promise upon obedience, and while a man sees or closes with no
more of the Gospel, the Gospel is but a legall doctrine to him, it's not
the Gospel, he sees not the love declared, the glad tidings of Gods
good will to him a sinner and ungodly in the gift of Jesus: in the belief of which he should be principled to the thing required: but I say
thou meeting with such a conditionall promise, thou endeavourest after faith, and humility, and fruits, and from thy self-endeavours, changes and self differings, which thou thinkest are notable fruits of faith,
thou concludest and trustest in thy self, that thou art righteous, a
believer, a justifyed one, and so that Christ is thy Mediatour, and died
for thee, and attributest this to God as if thou wert no enemy to grace,
but a Preacher of it in opposition to free-will, and thus many men do
whenas they never yet saw or discerned what grace is, nor had any o-
ther principle in what they did, but the law, its threats and promises,
and their own will; whence though they have as strong confidence of
their being righteous as the Pharisee had, yet it is but a strong fancy
and groundlesse conception of faith, the bottom of it is a legall cove-
nant, and their own work and endeavour, not the word of the Gospel, the declaration of grace, they receive not the word that should
beget it. I know they say they beleeve all the Scriptures, from the beginning of *Genesis* to the latter end of the *Revelations*, but come to the
point, let us examine thee in the testimony of God, whereof the Apostle *Paul* was made a Preacher, a Crier, or Herauld for the obedience of
faith, we finde it 1 *Tim.*2.4,5,6,7.Dost thou beleeve this ? God wils all
men to be saved, and come to the knowledge of the truth : and that
Christ gave himself a ransome for all, *&c.* by and by they crie out, A
damnable heresie, I see it there written, but I am not perswaded it is
meant as it was spoken, I cannot embrace it : Well, how then ? God
hath good will to none but an elect number in the world, Christ gave
himself a ransome for no other. Where readest thou that ? not such a
word in all the Bible : well, but how knowest thou then for thy self ?
thou wilt say, God forbid that I should not think that Christ died for
me: Why so, if not for all ? yes, I hope so (will the very drunkards say,
though they deny it for all) Every one will flatter himself in a good
conceit of himself, and make his own good conceit the ground of his
faith, and so the faith proves thereafter, but the most generall plea is,
I am thus humbled, changed, *&c.* as if he should say, God I thank thee
I am not as other men are : Now though they say, they beleeve for
themselves that that is in it self true, yet, this being not the effect of
the word of the Gospel in them, but a conclusion drawn by themselves
from their own changes or self-flattery, it hath not the nature of divine

vine faith in it, but of opinion : and what good works they do or seem to do, they are not fruits of the word of God working through faith in them, and so not the lively evidences of faith, but things endeavoured after by the power of law and conscience in them, to annex and pinne them to their faith, or rather to maintain and uphold their own opinion of their having faith. Too many Preachers there are that are in the fault, for building up men in this manner, not preaching the word of Gods grace to them, according to the tenour of the Apostolicall commission, some of whom while they plead for unity, in the mean time depart from the unity of the faith, and will not strive together with us, for that tenour of it once delivered to the Saints, but have made a division besides and contrary to that wholsome doctrine, whereas all unity should stand in verity, and then it will be lasting unity : oh that they would beleeve the word of God, that it may appear that the power and force thereof operates in them, and that their faith and works spring therefrom, and we are ready to embrace unity with them : yea, in the mean time we will love them and be at unity with them in what they had according to the word, though we must reprove them, when they disclaim, dissent, and draw people from the credit of the word, as if our reproving their strayings from that, or holding forth the word as we finde and beleeve it faithfully to the people, make or occasion division, we cannot help that, we must not lay down the truth of God to gain peace with men. Let men lay aside opposition then to the Gospel-declaration, and if they hold it not forth, yet deny it not, disclaim not against it, oppose not evident Scripture-sayings, and we shall readily endeavour to be at one with them. Many deal with men as *Pharaohs* officers with the poor Israelites, they took away the straw, and yet required the tale of brick, so men now presse men upon faith and repentance, and yet in the mean while withhold from them the doctrine of Gods love and goodnesse : to what purpose is it to tell men of the priviledges of beleevers, and withhold from them, or render doubtfull to them those motives of Gods good will toward them and Christs death for them, which God in the Gospel holds forth to them to bring them to believe ? to what purpose talk ye to men out of Christ, and uncalled, of a secret election that is only in Christ, and no where else to be met with nor enjoied, suppressing the doctrine of the death of Christ for them, that should draw them unto Christ, and tell them stories of an eternall reprobation, without respect to their

Phil. 1.17. *Rom.16.17.*

Maledicta sit illa charitas propter quam periclitatur vel amittitur veritas. Luth.

D rejecting

rejecting Gods grace : yea, with an affirmation that there was no such grace for the greater part of mankinde to be received or rejected by them, as is affirmed in the Gospel for them : so obstructing the way of their apprehending that grace that should leade them to repentance, or to put them upon a form of repentance, that hath no power in it, that they might presume themselves elect (for better it cannot be) while the doctrine of Gods grace and goodnesse is not held forth and magnified toward them, which leadeth to a true and living repentance and faith of Gods elect.

2. Again, how many talk of faith, and yet shew no fruits of faith? *Qui Curios simulant & Bacchanalia vivunt,* call themselves Christians but neither have the anointing, nor do the works of Christianity, that professe the Gospel, yet rest in the letter or shell of it, and look not into it to behold the glorious grace discovered in the Gospel, nor embrace the reproofs of self and flesh, fleshly wisedom, strength, righteousnesse and affections that come along to them in and with the Gospel, that talk of grace, but receive it in vain, and yeeld not up the inmost of their hearts to grace, welcome it not in its teachings to deny ungodlinesse and worldly lust, and to live soberly, righteously and godly in this present world, receive not the love of the truth to be saved by it from Satans temptations, and their own corruptions, thou saist thou believest and hopest to have heaven and happinesse, but yet thou art a drunkard, a whoremaster, a blasphemer, covetous, thy works proclaim thee to be a lyar, such faith as consists in opinion, and saying thou believest, and yet hath no power in thee to break thee off from vanities, will never save thee from destruction. It's true, Saints have had their failings, but they have been but failings, and they have been saved out of them, they have not lain and wallowed in their sin, and yet said, tush, these are but failings, their failings and fallings through temptation can be no plea for thee, that never yet arose from sin, and that livest and sportest thy self in thy sin. O deceive not thy self with a vain conception, to think the outward profession of a Christian will save thee, when nothing of his divine power and spirit dwels within thee, turn not the grace of God into lasciviousnesse, backslide not from the escapes you have had from pollutions through the knowledge of Christ to be intangled again with your corruptions, and yet flatter up your selves with the Saints failings, and say, ye may be true believers and reall Saints for all this: thou saiest thou seekest a countrey too, an heavenly city, and yet thy care is altogether for, and thy love eager to this

countrey, how to live bravely, and fare deliciously, uphold thy name and reputation, with men, though by vanity and iniquity, misse no advantages of grasping in the world to thy self, of satisfying thy affections, and enjoying thy vain pleasures, &c. sure these are not the works of faith, thou walkest not as the good old Patriarchs who counted themselves strangers and pilgrims in the earth, and regarded not to return to their own countrey, which they came out of at Gods commandment; as the former sort of men deny the word of faith, and discover their defect of faith by opposition to the word, so these by their works declare the vanity of their words: neither of these faiths, faith upon works and not grounded on and springing from the word, nor faith (or rather a saying a man hath faith) without works (inward operations and outward testimonies through the power of the word feeding it) will suffice to make a man just, or cause him to live, nor will either of them be sufficient for dying to keep a man that he see not death. But there's one thing more yet, *they received not the promises, though they beleeved and saw them afar off*: they died in faith, but yet enjoyed them not: how may we understand that, and what shall we note from it? The promises metonymically for the things promised, which are either for this life or the life that is to come; for this life, such as these to be a shield to them, to protect them, provide for them, give them children, &c. for the life to come, such as the countrey or city that hath foundations, the full enjoyment of himself and his glory: and as the way to that, the Messias to be born of their seed, to die and rise, &c. as also to blesse all nations in him.

Again, the word [*promise*] sometimes in Scripture signifies the word of promise, or the promise it self made in words to us, and by these distinctions and considerations we may resolve a doubt, for whereas it's said here, *these all died in faith, not having received the promises*, it's said, as we reade it in *ver.* 17. that *Abraham* had received the promise, *He that had received the promises offered up his only begotten Son,* and so *chap.* 6. 15. *after he had patiently endured he obtained the promise.* The solution, that the word of a promise he had received from God, God made his promise with and to him, and that promise as a thing made in word, he had received it, he heard it and beleeved it, but he had not received the things spoken of in that promise, or in those promises, as the word promises in the text signifies the things promised.

2. He did before he died obtain and receive the promise in some

things

things but not in all, the promiſes for this life of having God a
ſhield to him to protect him and be his God, and own him and
give him a Sonne, theſe he had obtained and received before he
died, yea, before he offered up his ſon *Iſaac*, but not all the promiſes, nor the main things promiſed, as neither the land of *Ca-*
naan, nor the multiplying his ſeed as the ſtars of heaven, nor
the Meſſias coming and bleſſing all nations, nor (which is the
main, the full thing aimed at) the heavenly countrey or kingdome, the enjoyment of God and Chriſt in glory with his ſeed,
and yet theſe they were heirs of, theſe fell to them by lot from
God, *Heb.*6.12. yea, theſe they received *in ſemine*, in *Iſaac*, and
Iſaac in *Iacob*, &c. they had them *in pignore*, but not *in plenitu-*
dine, in the firſt fruits or pledge, but not in the full enjoyment,
They all died in faith not having received the promiſes, the greateſt
part, the glory and the inheritance promiſed they received not,
and yet though they had them not till their death, yet they left not
off believing and hoping for them, nay, in their very death they
held faſt that faith and hope of them, and that upheld them in
death, they knew themſelves heirs of them, and judged God faithfull not to deprive them. But how could that be, ſeeing now they
died without them? Sure then they looked for another day and
time in which they ſhould enjoy them, and in which we alſo that
now believe ſhould enjoy them with them, as is ſaid, *ver.* 39, 40.
Theſe all being witneſſed of by faith, or having received a good re-
port or teſtimony by faith, received not the promiſes, God having pro-
vided ſome better thing for us, that they without us ſhould not be made
perfect. God hath provided another time and day, in which they and
we together ſhall receive and enjoy them: Mnde we here then a
little: theſe dying beleeved ſtill the receit of the promiſes, though
even at the time of their death they had not received them: how
did they then believe, wrong or right? was the thing they believed true or falſe? Surely their faith was good, for the holy Ghoſt
here commends it, and God therefore vouchſafed to be called
their God, having prepared a city for them, *verſ.* 16. and if ſo,
then ſurely they muſt yet have the promiſes performed to them
though now dead. What ſhall we ſay then? Verily we muſt needs
hence further note,

That there ſhall be a reſurrection from the dead, death ſhall not fru-
ſtrate the promiſes of God, and make void their faith.

There ſhall be a time when they ſhall be brought out of the
power of death and grave, and then ſhall receive the promiſes

that

that they died fhort of: then fhall the word of God be performed to them: and indeed here was the triumph of their faith: that
though God kill them and take their lives from them, and they
never fee the fulfilling of the prime things promifed, yet they beleeved that they fhould receive them: death it felf, wherein according to fenfe, there was an end put to them, and all further hope
and expectation, could not make their faith to fail them, *for they
beleeve in God that raifed the dead, and calleth things that are not
as if they were,* Rom.4 17. and fo above *hope beleeved in hope, according* (not to fenfe, but) *to what was fpoken of God, fo fhall thy
feed be.* O the power and vertue of divine faith, fupported by the
power of God in the belief of the refurrection from the dead!
Surely if they beleeved not in vain, as without doubt they did not,
then it undeniably follows that they fhall have (and fo that there
is) a day of Refurrection, when the promifed countrey and glory
fhall be made good unto them. Verily if this doctrine were not
true, our faith were vain, and the Gofpel preaching with its promifes vain, we could have no ground for faith in death, but faith
and hope and all muft die with us: but now they died all in
faith though they had not yet received the promifes: verily there
fhall be a reward for the righteous, for all their faith and patience: verily there fhall then be a refurrection of them that they
may be rewarded: the time of the *refurrection of the juft* is the
time of their *remuneration,* as in *Luk.*14.14. *Thou fhalt be rewarded in the refurrection of the juft:* deny the *refurrection* of the juft,
and thou takeft away the hope of their *reward,* and thou makeft
them of all men moft miferable, becaufe here they have a time
of deeper fufferings and forrowings then others, and thou telleft
them that they muft never rife more to receive a reward for
them, here they die, and have not received the promifes, and if
death fwallow them up, and they never rife, they muft never receive them: Look to this, you that deny the refurrection, I know
your evafion, you fay they have it already, they are in Chrift, and
rifen with him, and he is the refurrection and the life, and fo they
have their reward: but hearken thou vain man, though they be rifen with Chrift in their fpirits, rifen from earth to heaven, yet this
is not all their refurrection, nor have they herein their reward,
their full reward: for thus *Abraham* was raifed in his fpirit to
look after the heavenly countrey, even before he died (as they
that are raifed with Chrift in their fpirits are exhorted to feek the
things above, *Col.*3.1,2.) but yet even after that he died in faith,

and

and had not received the promises, he neither was raised above
faith to live without any further exercise of faith (as some vainly
prate) nor had he or any of them received all the reward of
faith, but they all died in faith not having received the promises,
and therefore must have yet another resurrection, or a compleat-
ing of that resurrection in the redemption of their bodies, that
they may receive those promises, according to that *Rom.* 8. 23.
We that have received the first-fruits of the spirit, yet wait for the a-
doption, the redemption of our bodies : for indeed the promises are
to the man, the whole man : now a man is not a man without his
body too, the soul is but part of the man (nay as *Tertullian* hath
well noted, the body is rather called the man, because it first had
the denomination of man : *God formed man of the dust of the earth,*
and breathed into him the breath of life, he was called man before
the breath of life was breathed into h'm, *Gen.* 2.7.) therefore the
resurrection is of that also, that must be raised and united to the
soul, that so the man may inherite the promise made to him : yea,
what is resurrection, but a raising to life that that died ? but the
spirits of just men die not with their bodies, they were raised up
and enlivened before, and live by faith even when the body dies,
therefore its the body must be raised, *He shall change our vile body,*
and make it like his own glorious body, Phil.3.21. yea, not the righteous only but the wicked too must rise, *Act.* 24.15. *There shall be a*
resurrection of the dead, both of the just and of the unjust. Heark you
Allegoriarum nimium amantes, nimium amentes, you that dote on
All gories, where will you finde ground of Allegory for this ? will
ye say the unjust and wicked too have Christ, and are risen with
Christ ? perhaps you will say, they shall rise from sinne to righteousnesse, and so into and with Christ, but (beside that this
crosseth the Scripture, all shall not so rise) you make that the resurrection of the just, and if that shall be the unjusts resurrection,
then I pray, what is that that's further spoken of, of the just seeing
that they have already, and yet speaking in the future tense, he
saith, *they shall arise ?* but what need we many words, when ou
Saviour is so expresse in *Joh.*5,29. *All that are in their graves shal*
bear the voice of the Son of man, and come forth, they that have don
good unto the resurrection of life, and they that have done evil unt
the resurrection of condemnation : not from sinne to righteousness
in this life, but to condemnation for their unrighteousnesse a
ed in this life. But we need not go so far from the text, to prov
that there shall be a resurrection of the body. Seeing by th

Hominem pro-
prie carnem di-
cit, quia vocabu-
lum hominis oc-
cupavit.

that here follows *that God is not ashamed to be called their God,* ver. 16. our Saviour hath to our hands confuted that opinion of the Sadduces, and proved that there shall be a resurrection even of them that are dead in the body: for that was the thing that the Sadduces oppugned, and not the quickning up of mens spirits to God, as we may see by their way of arguing, *Mar.*12.18,27. Then it is at that glorious resurrection that all things shall be made new, when the bodies that are dead shall by the power of God be raised, new heavens and new earth prepared, and given unto the Saints, in which dwels righteousnesse, that is, then shall they have and enjoy remainingly the righteousnesse of God in the full accomplishment of all his former promises, in the faith of which they died, but had not received.

Dear friends, hold fast this doctrine of the resurrection, for as *Tertullian* well begins his book upon this subject, *Fiducia Christianorum, resurrectio mortuorum,* the resurrection of the dead is the hope and expectation of Christians, there is no doctrine more properly Christian then it, none more comfortable, none now in greater danger to be let slip, these being those shaking times of the most fundamentall doctrines of Christian truth, which the Apostle *Peter* long since warned us of, 2 *Pet.*3.2,3,13. *There shall* (saies he) *come mockers, walking after their own ungodly lusts, that shall mock at the performance of Gods promises, in the coming of Christ, and restitution of all things, saying, where is the promise of his coming? for since the fathers fell asleep, all things continue in their state.* As if they should say, they are like to receive no more then they had before they died: but let not this doctrine be shaken from you, for what then will follow but a totall falling off from the faith, a denying of the resurrection of Christ, and of the kingdome of Christ? yea, then *faith and preaching and all is vain,* yea, then the reins are given to all licentiousnesse, *Let us eat and drink, for to morrow we shall die,* and when we are dead, there is a finall end with us, and that's indeed the issue of that wickednesse, they that say, *where is the promise of his coming? Will not fear to walk after their own ungodly lusts:* It's true, one principle upon which they lean in denying it, and way to insinuate the sleighting of it unto others (as *Tertullian* hath long since observed, and as experience of their words yet teacheth us) is a disrespect they seem to bear to the flesh, so our spirits enjoy God (say they) and go up to God, what's matter for this flesh? it's but dust, and to dust let it go, and no matter whether ever it rise

Applic.

1 Cor. 11.17, 18.

or

or not, but as he also well observes, *Sunt tamen carnis amicissimi,*
nemo enim tam carnaliter vivit, quam qui resurrectionem mortuo-
rum negat, though they seem to slieght the flesh, none love better
to please the flesh, none live more after the flesh: praiers and
ordinance and discipline then is nothing with them, to trim up
themselves, and wear, and eat, and drink the best, to play and
game (and perhaps do worse things) these they will not deny
the flesh, they will please it what they can here, because they think
it shall have no pleasure, or good hereafter. But oh! take heed
to the Scriptures, both Pharisees and Sadduces erre in not know-
Mat.22.29. ing and believing them: *ye erre, not knowing the Scriptures, nor the*
power of God: they pretend to know them better then others,
while they can pervert them more then others: and while they
pretend a more spirituall understanding of them, they contradict
the spirit of understanding speaking in them, and through fraud
and subtlety seduce the simple, seeming at first to speak as they,
till they winde them into their snares, as *Tertullian* observed of
De Res. Car. them in his times, they would say to the simple-hearted, *Væ qui*
in hâc carne non resurrexerint, Wo to them that rise not in this
flesh, which the simple-hearted hearing oftentimes were led to
judge they meant honestly and according to the Scripture only,
whenas they meant (saies he) *Dum in hâc carne sunt,* that rise
not while they are in this flesh, and so by one part of truth seem-
ingly confessed the rising of our spirits here by faith with Christ,
they would by little and little undermine the faith of the simple-
hearted, and doctrinate them not to matter, and then to deny
the resurrection of the body, running themselves and them that
listened to them into the errour of *Hymenæus* and *Philetus,* 2 Tim.
2.17. that say, *the resurrection is already past,* in whose very footsteps many also now walk, not knowing the Scriptures, yea, de-
parting from the Scriptures, and not acknowledging the power
of God: thence say they, how should the bodies that are long since
dead, and divers waies dispersed, and that have endured so many
transmutations be possibly raised? and how can the world it self
contain them? as if they did not believe God Almighty, and that
all things are possible to him beyond our thought, to whom I
might say with the Apostle *Act.*26 8. *Why should it be thought a*
thing incredible with you, that God should raise the dead? But I say
again, minde we the word of God, and so minde and keep it that
we may be kept by it in the faith from this dangerous errour of
the wicked, dream not with them of all our resurrection here: no
coming

coming of Chrift but what they meet with here, no performance
of promifes but what they have here, all enjoyments and fullneffe
and perfection here : fure if that was true *Paul* was very low and
ignorant to them, when he faies *he had finifhed his courfe, and kept*   2 Tim. 4 8.
the faith, and yet adds, *henceforth is laid up for me the crown of righ-*
teoufneffe, which God the righteous Judge fhall give me at that day : he
had done his work, and yet he had not received his reward : it was
but *laid up* for him, and laid up to be given him, not in *this* but in
that day, in another day, the day of Chrifts appearance, fure then
the Apoftle was out here too, when he faid, thefe all died in faith,
and yet had not received the promifes. Nay, the Apoftle *Paul* in-
ftructs us, that we fhall not one prevent another in the receit of
them, 1 *Thef. 4.* 15. *They that live at the coming of Chrift fhall not*
prevent them that are afleep : They that now live fhall not have them
till *Abraham, Ifaac* and *Jacob* have them, nor they before we have
them, *Heb.* 11. 40. the dead in Chrift fhall be firft raifed at his coming, and the living changed, and both be caught into the air up
together to meet him, certainly they fay falfe then that fay Chrift
is come to them in his glory, and they are raifed and have the promifes, all they look for, or all that any fhall have, and yet many of
their brethren died without them, and are not yet raifed, and if we
will believe them never fhall be, and many yet are uncalled to them.
But beloved, regard we not their fayings, but know them to be
falfe and vain, and look we to Chrift that died for us and rofe a-
gain, and know that as he rofe, fo fhall we alfo, and together with
Abraham and the Patriarchs and Prophets, and all the Saints fhall
be caught up at his appearance to meet him, as the Apoftle exhorts   1 Thef 4. 18
us, comfort we one another for our deceafed brethren with thefe
fayings. And indeed what comfort could we have for one another
in refpect of them, if we believed that all their portion they are to
have, they have had it already, and when they and we die, our fpirits go to God, and our bodies to the duft, and ther's an end of the
matter, we fhall never enjoy them again, there fhall be no refurrection ; away with fuch unchriftian and unfavoury conceptions, and
let us where we have believed hold faft the faith, and not upon any
pretence or by any Philofophy or vain deceit of man, depart therefrom, let us live in it, that we may die in it, or according to it.
  And thus I have given you a view of the text, I fuppofe you expect I
fhould now return to our prefent occafion, and fay fomething about
our deceafed brother : Truly the text is fuch a comment on him,
as that we might go over it again and apply it to him, or you might

E   under-

understand that spoken of these Worthies here, as if said of him, he believed the Gospel, and had insight in it, and oftentimes rejoiced much in it, was perswaded of it, embraced it, loved it, counted himself a stranger and pilgrim in the earth, walkt with that contempt and carelessnesse of it (how it thought of him and esteemed him) as if he judged it not his habitation, but had his eye (as indeed he had) upon a better countrey, an enduring city that hath foundations, he lived in this world as if he had his heart in another world, not regarding, nor scarce suffering the honours of this world or of this place to be thrust upon him; his name was nothing to him for the Gospels sake, that he would approve whoever disproved him, he would stop his ears against, and not endure to hear of their sayings, who deny Chrifts mediation, and impugn the doctrine of the resurrection, and professing his joy and comfort to be therein, and in the hope he had therethrough of an enduring happy condition: for juftice, uprightnesse and honefty, it was his aim and endeavour, and therein hath not left many to exceed (I doubt I may say to e-quallize) him, we may say of him, *the righteous man is taken away, and the mercifull man from amongst us*: In both which respects I fear many will misse him, as the loins of the poor blessed him alive, so I doubt they will finde cause of mourning for his death: as he affected not honour with men, so did he not long enjoy it, God not judging us worthy the improvement of his abilities for the good of the Town, perhaps because no better respected (when more able) by them: he was more like the self-denying Olive, then the aspiring bramble: he looked upon earths honour as a burthen, having his chief desire upon that which is from heaven, therefore God hath taken him from his burthen to give him his desire: in a word he was upright in his life, faithfull to the truth to his death, patient under affliction (though long in great pain) and very desirous of his dissolution, that he might be with Chrift. Let it be ourcare to imitate him in these good steps, that with him and all those
who through faith and patience have looked after the promises of God, we may in due time
be raised up, and brought to inherit
them. I shall only adde an Epi-
taph upon him, and I shall
leave both you and him.
⁂

F I N I S.

AN EPITAPH.

QVi cum vixit erat Major, major moriendo eſt
  (Morte repurgatus) quam fuit ipſe prius.
Majeſtatis erat brevita cadaveris umbra,
  Vix ea majeſtas, illius umbra brevis :
Spe lætus, multum q̃, gemens mala publica, corpus
  Mandat humo, plenam numine cælo animam.

In Engliſh thus.

This man alive was May'r, now dead is more
  Advanc't (death bettring him) then heretofore
Short ſhade o'th corps of Royalty he was,
  That Royalty ſcarce ſhadowed what he was.
Who joy'd in hope, did publike woes condole,
  Left earth his corps, to heaven his gracefull ſoul.

FINIS.

CPSIA information can be obtained at www.ICGtesting.com
Printed in the USA
LVOW03s2307140415

434552LV00019B/883/P